IN GOD'S GREAT OUTDOORS

IN GOD'S GREAT OUTDOORS

DEVOTIONS FOR HIKERS, CAMPERS, & NATURE LOVERS

ROB SCHRADER

WIPF & STOCK · Eugene, Oregon

IN GOD'S GREAT OUTDOORS
Devotions for Hikers, Campers, and Nature Lovers

Copyright © 2023 Rob Schrader. All rights reserved. Except for brief quotations in critical publications or reviews, no part of this book may be reproduced in any manner without prior written permission from the publisher. Write: Permissions, Wipf and Stock Publishers, 199 W. 8th Ave., Suite 3, Eugene, OR 97401.

Wipf & Stock
An Imprint of Wipf and Stock Publishers
199 W. 8th Ave., Suite 3
Eugene, OR 97401

www.wipfandstock.com

PAPERBACK ISBN: 978-1-6667-5772-9
HARDCOVER ISBN: 978-1-6667-5773-6
EBOOK ISBN: 978-1-6667-5774-3

"Scripture quotations are from The ESV® Bible (The Holy Bible, English Standard Version®), copyright© 2001 by Crossway, a publishing ministry of Good News Publishers. Used by permission. All rights reserved."

The photographs were taken by either Austin Miller or Rob Schrader, as indicated. Used by permission. All rights reserved.

A big "Thank You" to my friend Austin Miller for allowing me to include his truly fantastic photography in this book.

If you would like to view his work or order prints, visit his website at:
https://austinmiller.photography/

TABLE OF CONTENTS

KEY
To read a specific devotion that addresses the environment you're currently in, use this key to interpret the symbols you'll find following each devotion in the table of contents below.

 Mountains   Forest   Desert   Water    General

Introduction	01	
Psalm 104	04	
1 - 🌐 Psalm 135:7	07	
2 - 🌲 2 Corinthians 4:16	09	
3 - 🏜 Matthew 10:42	11	
4 - 🌐 Psalm 63:1	13	
5 - 🌐 Proverbs 4:26-27	15	
6 - 🌐 Colossians 1:17	17	
7 - 🌐 1 Peter 5:6-7	19	
8 - 🌐 Genesis 8:22	21	
9 - 🌐 Exodus 3:8	23	
10 - ⛰ Matthew 7:14	25	
11 - 🌐 Psalm 8:3-4	27	
12 - 〰 John 4:13-14	29	
13 - 🌐 Mark 4:39	31	
14 - ⛰ Psalm 102:25-26	33	
15 - 🌐 John 14:6	35	
16 - 🌐 Matthew 7:24	37	
17 - 🌐 Philippians 2:3	39	
18 - ⛰ 1 Corinthians 9:25	41	
19 - 〰 Job 11:7, 9	43	
20 - 🌲 Psalm 29:5	45	
21 - 〰 Matthew 9:28-29	47	
22 - 🌐 Psalm 19:1	49	
23 - 🌐 Matthew 11:28	51	
24 - 🌐 Job 41:11	53	
25 - ⛰ Matthew 24:13	55	
26 - 🌐 Psalm 121:2	57	
27 - 🌐 Isaiah 11:6	59	
28 - 🌐 Ephesians 5:8	61	
29 - 🌲 Isaiah 40:28	63	
30 - 🌐 Psalm 103:11	65	
31 - ⛰ James 4:14	67	
32 - 🌐 Genesis 1:31	69	
33 - 🌐 Psalm 112:4	71	
34 - 🏜 Ephesians 2:4-5	73	
35 - 🌐 Psalm 95:4-5	75	
36 - 🏜 Jeremiah 17:7-8	77	
37 - 🌐 Psalm 29:4	79	
38 - 🌐 1 Peter 1:6-7	81	
39 - 🌐 Romans 1:16	83	
40 - ⛰ Judges 5:5	85	
Psalm 148	86	
Prayer	87	

INTRODUCTION

Hello! I'm glad and grateful that you've picked up this book! I suppose I should begin by introducing myself—I'm Rob. I'm a pastor and lover of the outdoors. I decided to write this little book when I couldn't find another small, easily packed devotional to accompany me on the trail and in the tent. There's nothing I love more than God and few things that I enjoy more than the outdoors, and the two go together like marshmallows and graham crackers, tents and sleeping bags, campfires and friends. With that in mind, I hope you find this collection of devotions to be a welcome companion that brings God and his word to your outdoor experience.

I called this book In God's Great Outdoors because the Bible teaches that the great outdoors do indeed belong to him. Scripture says that God created the earth and everything in it, as well as the universe all around us (Genesis 1-2). In fact, the existence of this universe and of you and me is one way that we can be certain God exists—everything could not have come from nothing. Not only does nature reveal God's existence, it also teaches us much about him—such lessons from the natural world are one of the things the devotions in this book try to bring out.

Although we can learn a lot about God from creation, the natural world can't, however, teach us everything we need to know about him. For this reason, God revealed himself to humanity in a more direct way—he spoke to us and even became one of us. I'm talking, of course, about Jesus (Hebrews 1:2). Without him, each and every one of us would be lost in our sins and going to hell. But with Jesus, we have assured hope for deliverance and heaven! How? Well, the Bible explains that Jesus lived the perfect life that we fail to live, yet he was convicted, he suffered, and he was crucified. On the cross, he took the punishment that we deserve in our place and, in so doing, forgave our sins! He died and was buried, but then he rose from the dead, defeated death, and now offers eternal life to all people! The Bible also reveals to us that the only way we can receive this incredible gift from God is through faith. "Faith" simply means trusting that Jesus's work really does redeem you from hell and grant you eternal life in heaven.

I wrote this book to join together God's two great revelations of himself. In God's Great Outdoors uses nature—a place where we encounter God and are convinced of his presence—to teach the eternally essential truths about him that can only be found in the Bible. It's in the great outdoors where many of us feel God and ponder God; it's out in his creation where we marvel and wonder at him. This book seeks to build on those feelings, thoughts, and experiences by teaching you, the reader more about God—especially his gracious love toward us in Jesus Christ.

And ultimately, it's faith in God's gracious love toward us that matters. Life isn't about how many mountains you've climbed or trails you've hiked. It's not about how many places you've been or sites you've seen. It's not even about connecting with nature or appreciating its beauty. Eventually, we all die, and then none of that matters; the old saying is true: "You can't take it with you when you go." In the end, the only thing that counts is faith. If you have faith in Jesus and what he has done for you, then God guarantees that you'll have eternal life in his amazing presence.

■ ■ ■ ■ ■ ■

In God's Great Outdoors is meant for both non-Christians and Christians alike. For the non-Christian, I hope that this book helps you learn about the one, true God who created the world all around you, and I pray that you'll want to know more about him. If the Holy Spirit sparks that in your heart, I recommend finding a Bible-believing church, attending, and getting involved. For the Christian reader, I hope that this book strengthens your faith. I pray that through these devotions you come to know God more fully and learn to see him and his great love all around you. I pray also that you'll perhaps pass on this book (or at least its teachings) to other lovers of the outdoors—Christians and non-Christians alike. Don't be afraid to share God's good news with those on the trail, in the campsite, or on the park bench next to you as you experience God and his great outdoors!

Before I go, I want to leave you with a note as to how I intended this book to be used (not as toilet paper, I hope, though if it's an emergency, I do understand!). Found within are forty short devotions that can easily be read during a water break, around a campfire, in a tent, at the park, on your front porch, or in any such location. As you will see, the entries are meant to be read outside (though with a little imagination, they can, of course, be read inside as well). I limited the number to forty to keep the book from being too cumbersome to take on the trail. As a result, In God's Great Outdoors is not intended to be used as a daily devotional but instead as one to be read whenever you're having an adventure.

In one sense, all of these devotions contain the same message of Jesus Christ and what he did on the cross because this is the central, essential teaching of Christianity (and since the texts aren't intended to be read daily, I didn't think the theme would become too redundant). At the same time, I did my best to proclaim this message in a unique way in each devotion; each entry contains different experiences, connections, thoughts, and teachings about Christianity. So, I would encourage you to read this whole book—one devotion at a time, one hike at a time, one campout at a time, one trip into the outdoors at a time. If you read the whole devotional, you won't have a complete understanding of God—no one does. But you will have a well-rounded understanding of who he is and what he has done for you—and that is the most important information any of us can know! I'd recommend beginning each devotion by reading the provided Bible verse that it's based on. Each entry concludes with a short prayer that also serves to sum up the main teaching of that devotion.

I'd like to thank you again for giving this little book a try, and I sincerely hope that you find it beneficial. I wish you great faith, God's blessings, and happy trails!

PSALM 104

¹ Bless the L<small>ORD</small>, O my soul!
    O L<small>ORD</small> my God, you are very great!
 You are clothed with splendor and majesty,
 ²   covering yourself with light as with a garment,
    stretching out the heavens like a tent.
³ He lays the beams of his chambers on the waters;
    he makes the clouds his chariot;
    he rides on the wings of the wind;
⁴ he makes his messengers winds,
    his ministers a flaming fire.

⁵ He set the earth on its foundations,
    so that it should never be moved.
⁶ You covered it with the deep as with a garment;
    the waters stood above the mountains.
⁷ At your rebuke they fled;
    at the sound of your thunder they took to flight.
⁸ The mountains rose, the valleys sank down
    to the place that you appointed for them.
⁹ You set a boundary that they may not pass,
    so that they might not again cover the earth.

¹⁰ You make springs gush forth in the valleys;
    they flow between the hills;
¹¹ they give drink to every beast of the field;
    the wild donkeys quench their thirst.
¹² Beside them the birds of the heavens dwell;
    they sing among the branches.
¹³ From your lofty abode you water the mountains;
    the earth is satisfied with the fruit of your work.

¹⁴ You cause the grass to grow for the livestock
    and plants for man to cultivate,
   that he may bring forth food from the earth
¹⁵ and wine to gladden the heart of man,
    oil to make his face shine
    And bread to strengthen man's heart.

¹⁶ The trees of the Lord are watered abundantly,
    the cedars of Lebanon that he planted.
¹⁷ In them the birds build their nests;
    the stork has her home in the fir trees.
¹⁸ The high mountains are for the wild goats;
    the rocks are a refuge for the rock badgers.
    and bread to strengthen man's heart.

¹⁹ He made the moon to mark the seasons;
    the sun knows its time for setting.
²⁰ You make darkness, and it is night,
    when all the beasts of the forest creep about.
²¹ The young lions roar for their prey,
    seeking their food from God.
²² When the sun rises, they steal away
    and lie down in their dens.
²³ Man goes out to his work
    and to his labor until the evening.

²⁴ O Lord, how manifold are your works!
    In wisdom have you made them all;
    the earth is full of your creatures.
²⁵ Here is the sea, great and wide,
    which teems with creatures innumerable,
    living things both small and great.
²⁶ There go the ships,
    and Leviathan, which you formed to play in it.

²⁷ These all look to you,
    to give them their food in due season.
²⁸ When you give it to them, they gather it up;
    when you open your hand, they are filled with good things.
²⁹ When you hide your face, they are dismayed;
    when you take away their breath, they die
    and return to their dust.
³⁰ When you send forth your Spirit, they are created,
    and you renew the face of the ground.

³¹ May the glory of the Lord endure forever;
    may the Lord rejoice in his works,
³² who looks on the earth and it trembles,
    who touches the mountains and they smoke!
³³ I will sing to the Lord as long as I live;
    I will sing praise to my God while I have being.
³⁴ May my meditation be pleasing to him,
    for I rejoice in the Lord.
³⁵ Let sinners be consumed from the earth,
    and let the wicked be no more!
    Bless the Lord, O my soul!
    Praise the Lord!

Mt. Baker, WA

Photo by: Austin Miller

PSALM 135:7

"He it is who makes the clouds rise at the end of the earth, who makes lightnings for the rain and brings forth the wind from his storehouses."

I don't know about you, but I'm the kind of guy who likes sitting out on the porch while it's storming. I'm even the kind of guy who likes sleeping in a tent while it's storming, provided that the tent doesn't leak! I love watching it lightning; I love listening to it rain and thunder. Strangely enough, to me there's something calming about it all. And there's something about a storm that reminds me of God.

The same can be said for the writer of Psalm 135. Overall, it's a great Psalm of praise to God for all the awesome things that he does, and one of those awesome things is storms. Whether you find them calming or terrifying, exciting or chilling—you must admit that a storm is an awe-inspiring sight. The sheer power and wonder of the elements are incredible: countless gallons of water falling from the heavens, huge bolts of electricity shooting across the sky, and the invisible air all around you moving with such force that it can uproot trees! There's so much energy and might in these natural wonders. However, the psalmist reminds us that God is even more powerful—he's the storm-bringer, the one who can control the elements of nature and even the one who created nature! The writer of Psalm 135 says to praise God for this incredible power of his. Certainly, you should! Though, other parts of the Psalm remind you to also praise God because he's a deliverer—he's *your* deliverer (Psalm 135:8–14). The one with the power to create storms has not used his power to destroy you. Instead, he has used his power to save you! Paul writes, "In him we have redemption through his blood, the forgiveness of our trespasses" (Ephesians 1:7). Though you deserve destruction because of your sinfulness, God instead has shown you mercy (Hebrews 4:16). In fact, he took your sin upon himself, and he endured the destruction you deserve as he died on the cross. Then by his great power, he rose from death to give all who believe in him a resurrection from death, too!

When you see a powerful storm, remember that God is even more mighty. But remember also his mercy: he used his power not to destroy but to deliver you!

Almighty Father, thank you for displaying your power in your great mercy toward me. Amen.

Door County, WI

Photo by: Rob Schrader

2 CORINTHIANS 4:16

"So we do not lose heart. Though our outer self is wasting away, our inner self is being renewed day by day."

The springtime is one of my favorite times to hike. The forest, once colored only in various shades of gray, becomes a tapestry of color! In fact, all the various hues seem brightest this time of year. You can't help but smile as green shoots sprout from the earth, blossoms appear on the trees, and bushes begin to bud. It's not only the sights but also the smells and the sounds—the fresh air, the cheerful chirping of birds, the scurrying of squirrels among the trees. The world wakes up from its long winter slumber. Each and every day more growth appears—gradually each portion of the forest comes alive!

In the springtime, you could say that the forest is being renewed day by day. This is what Paul wrote in Second Corinthians about Christians. Just as the forest appears dead during the winter, so also all people are dead. Though we walk and talk, eat and drink, live and think, without God, we're really on borrowed time. You may live for a hundred years, but eventually you'll die—that's certain. As Paul says, "Our outer self is wasting away"—every day brings death closer. This death is a result of our sinfulness: "You were dead in the trespasses and sins in which you once walked" (Ephesians 2:1-2). But our death is not what God wants; he created you to live forever! So, God came to the world as Jesus and gave his own life on the cross so that humanity might again have eternal life (Romans 5:10). This gift is received through faith: simply by trusting in God to give you eternity, you have exactly that!

So, if you're Christian, though each day brings you closer to bodily death, it also brings you closer to true life, to eternal life! You are renewed day by day—your daily sins are daily forgiven, and eternal life is daily yours. Just as a spring forest shows more life with each passing day, so also does the believer in Christ. As you observe the cycle of the seasons, see it as a metaphor for your life. You will die. But, thanks to God, if you have faith in him, you'll also be renewed to live in heaven forever!

Gracious Redeemer, I thank you for renewing me day by day and giving me eternal life. Amen.

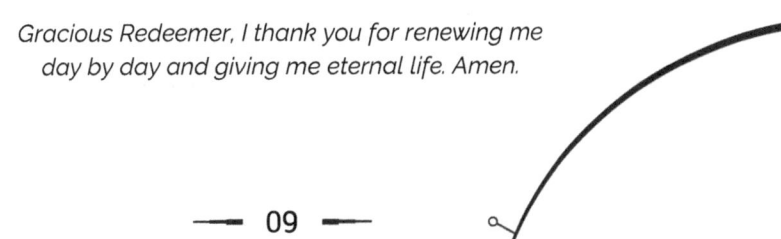

Yellowstone Natl. Park, WY

Photo by: Austin Miller

MATTHEW 10:42

"And whoever gives one of these little ones even a cup of cold water because he is a disciple, truly, I say to you, he will by no means lose his reward."

Have you ever run out of water while hiking or backpacking? I have. I was backpacking in the desert, and I'd fallen and had to use quite a bit of water to clean some cuts I had gotten. I only had one bottle left, was already feeling dehydrated, and had a long hike back out in the morning. Unbeknownst to me, I'd set up camp near a 4x4 road. Entirely by the grace of God, a large group drove that road and set up their camp about one hundred yards away; they had a truck full of water! Graciously, they gave me as much as I wanted.

It's kindness like this that Jesus teaches about in Matthew 10. He talks about Christians living out their faith through acts of service—even small ones like giving someone a cup of water. Christians are to serve other people because Jesus has served the world (1 John 4:11). He went far beyond giving a cup of water, though; he gave something much more valuable: his life! The immortal God died, so that mortal men could become immortal (1 Corinthians 15:53 and 1 Peter 1:23). He then rose back to life, and by his resurrection, he grants this immortality to all who believe this! His resurrection demonstrates to and assures the world that he is God, that he has power over death, and that through faith in him, you'll also have a resurrection. Paul explains, "He who raised Christ Jesus from the dead will also give life to your mortal bodies through his Spirit who dwells in you" (Romans 8:11).

The water I received on that hot, desert day was wonderfully quenching, but it's nowhere near as incredible or refreshing as Jesus' gift of eternal life. Having refreshed us in this most wonderful way, Jesus teaches his followers to go out and refresh others. You could do this by giving a cup of cold water, providing for the poor, lifting up the lowly, helping the hurting, telling others the wonderful news of Jesus, or doing so many other things. He promises that those who have this faith that is living and active "will by no means lose [their] reward." That reward is the gift of a resurrection to eternal life! Live refreshed by this promise.

Refreshing Redeemer, thank you for serving me; help me to refresh others. Amen.

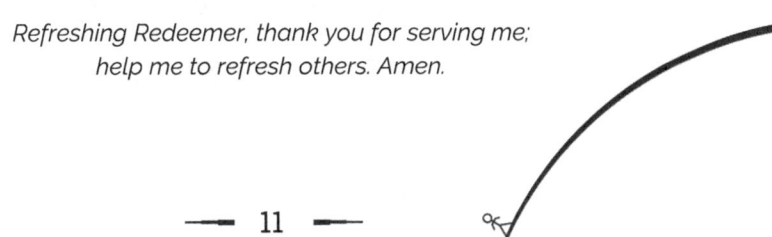

Glacier Natl. Park, MT

Photo by: Austin Miller

PSALM 63:1

"O God, you are my God; earnestly I seek you; my soul thirsts for you; my flesh faints for you, as in a dry and weary land where there is no water."

Confidently, you start your hike. Things are going great! Then, there's an unmapped fork. Or the trail becomes hard to follow. Or you realize you brought the wrong map! Slowly, fear and worry start to creep in—you're lost! I've experienced those scenarios so many times; most often the danger was minimal, but occasionally the situation was somewhat serious. In those moments the only thing that seems to matter is finding someone who isn't lost. Earnestly, you begin to seek help.

This common hiking scenario relates to many lives. If you don't know God, you're lost. You may be walking, but you really don't know where you're going to end up. At times, I have to admit that I've forgotten about God. Have you? It usually happens when things are going great; it's then that he tends to slip from one's mind (Hosea 13:6). At these times, God often uses suffering to get your attention once again, to humble you, and to remind you that you're ultimately lost without him (2 Chronicles 33:12). As in the hiking analogy above, he hopes that as a result of your difficulty you'll earnestly seek him: the one who is the way to true joy, peace, and everlasting life. This is what David was experiencing as he wrote Psalm 63. He was in the Judean wilderness running for his life because an evil king was after him. David had nowhere to turn but to the Lord, and turn he did! In a great example for you to follow, he earnestly sought God. For those who do this, God promises, "Seek, and you will find" (Matthew 7:7). Truly, finding God is the highest good! For when you have faith in him, then you have the only thing that ultimately matters: the gift of eternal life in heaven!

I'm sure you don't like to suffer. But, when you do, remember that God has a bigger picture in mind. He often uses temporary suffering on earth to draw you to him so that he can save you from eternal suffering in hell. With that in mind, when you suffer, turn to God for help. He wants to use that suffering so that you'll seek him, rely on him, and have faith in him—so that you'll have him and, ultimately, the end of all suffering, eternally (2 Corinthians 4:8-10).

God, thank you for drawing me to you; help me to always seek you. Amen.

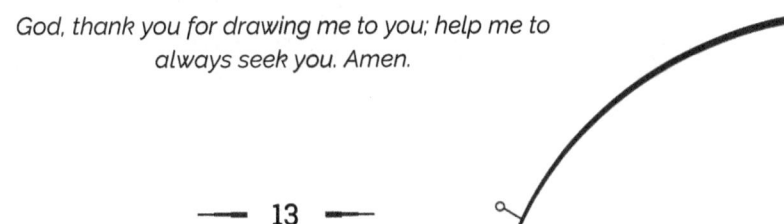

Mt. Rainier Natl. Park, WA

Photo by: Austin Miller

PROVERBS 4:26-27

"Ponder the path of your feet; then all your ways will be sure. Do not swerve to the right or to the left; turn your foot away from evil."

In Israel, east of the Sea of Galilee, lie mountains known as the Golan Heights. This is disputed territory that separates Israel from Syria, and it's often been the location of fighting between these two nations. On an archaeological trip to Israel, I hiked in that area a few times. It's very beautiful, very hot, and for those who venture off the path—very dangerous. In many places there are signs that read: "Danger: Mines." Though I often enjoy wandering off-trail, knowing that I might encounter a land mine kept me stuck to the path like glue!

This "sticking to the path" is what Solomon writes about in Proverbs 4, though he isn't talking about hiking. Instead, Solomon speaks about life. He says, "Ponder the path of your feet"; in other words, think about where you're going. Is your ultimate destination heaven? If that's where you'd like to end up (and since it's far better than the alternative, I assume it is), are you actually on the right path? The Bible explains that there's only one way to heaven and that's through faith in Jesus Christ (Acts 4:12). Solomon's next piece of advice is for those already on that path: "Do not swerve to the right or to the left; turn your foot away from evil." In this life, it's easy to be enticed off the trail by sinful lusts and to find yourself in a minefield. The devil uses things like sex, money, popularity, and pleasure to lead you away from God (Luke 8:14). Though not bad in themselves, if you make these things your "god" and leave the true path by walking after them, you'll find yourself in a danger far worse than a minefield. Land mines can only kill the body, but leaving God's path and pursuing sin results in eternal death in hell (Matthew 10:28). That's why God gives laws—they're a curb that keeps you focused on him and walking on his path to paradise.

God's law is a sign that reads, "Danger: Mines." It's meant to help you avoid running after the things that lead to hell. By the power of the Holy Spirit, recognize sin for what it is, and instead keep your focus on the God, who promises eternal life to all who stay on his path.

Heavenly Guide, thanks for giving me a path to heaven; help me to remain on it. Amen.

Yosemite Natl. Park, CA

Photo by: Austin Miller

COLOSSIANS 1:17

"And he is before all things, and in him all things hold together."

06

I've been blessed to have hiked in all kinds of climates and terrains. One thing I continually find amazing whenever I go to harsher regions is the amount of growth and life found there. Personally, I can't keep a house plant alive, yet I see trees growing on rocky mountains with little soil, shrubs and cacti flourishing in dry deserts, and grass covering hot, wind-swept plains. It's truly a miracle that life exists and even thrives all over this planet, even in the harshest, most improbable places.

That's a testament to God. The all-intelligent Creator designed a huge variety of plants and animals so that his earth would be covered with life. In fact, he's so brilliant that he even built into living things the ability to adapt so that as environments change, life continues to thrive. Coming from someone who can't grow a flower in a flowerpot, I'm amazed by the power of God to grow and sustain life all over this planet (Psalm 145:15–16). Indeed, "In him all things hold together." He loves life, and he continues to provide for its needs so that it flourishes! Isn't he incredible? While God loves all life, the pinnacle of his creation is human beings. He loves mankind so much that he created us to have eternal life. But we sin. And Paul explains, "Death spread to all men because all sinned" (Romans 5:12). Yet, just as God sustains life all over this planet, he executed a plan to sustain the eternal life of humanity. The Bible tells the story of this plan; it culminates in Jesus Christ. He came to earth in order "to give his life as a ransom for many" (Mark 10:45). Since it's your sins that bring you death, Jesus took all of your sins upon himself while hanging on the cross, and by dying, he paid their ransom price (Colossians 1:21–22). In paying that price, he frees you from death and hell and offers you a restoration to eternal life. Three days after dying, Jesus rose from the dead, proving he's God and that he really has saved you from death. God's plan worked; he is victorious!

God is truly a lover of life. Not only does he continually provide for life all over this earth, but he's also provided eternal life to all those who believe in him. Knowing this about God, trust in him and receive from him abundant life now and forever.

Creator and Sustainer, thank you for providing for me in this life and the next. Amen.

Glacier Natl. Park, MT

Photo by: Austin Miller

1 PETER 5:6-7

"Humble yourselves, therefore, under the mighty hand of God so that at the proper time he may exalt you, casting all your anxieties on him, because he cares for you."

On every backpacking trip someone inevitably complains about the heaviness of their pack. Multiday hiking trips have a compounded effect—people complain about their sore feet, the hot sun, the mosquitoes, and so on. Admittedly, I've done my fair share of complaining. What about you? While most of the time I love it, hiking can be uncomfortable and difficult. I'd be lying if I said I've loved every moment of every hike.

This difficult, challenging life is very similar. Surely, you've experienced seasons of suffering—sickness and injury, broken relationships, loss, or discontentment. Sometimes you get sore shoulders from carrying a heavy load of responsibility, guilt, or shame. Sometimes your feet hurt as you navigate the rocky road of life, tripping and stumbling along the way. Other times, it's the "mosquitoes"—you're just pestered and annoyed. The Bible explains that this suffering is a result of all of the sin that we all do (Genesis 3:16-19). And even though we deserve to suffer because we sin, God still uses suffering to our benefit. For instance, so often when people aren't suffering, they forget about God, so God uses suffering to remind them that they need him. For when a person trusts in God, then they have everything good, and this is what God wants for us (1 Peter 4:13). Additionally, Paul explains that Christians are "heirs with Christ, provided we suffer with him in order that we may also be glorified with him" (Romans 8:17). In this, you can also see a second way that God uses suffering to your benefit—through his own suffering (Hebrews 12:2). He came to this uncomfortable earth and endured the punishment you deserve for your immorality as he died on the cross, forsaken by God. Then he overcame death, the ultimate suffering, so that you can also have a resurrection like him.

When you suffer, trust in your suffering savior. In humility, cast your anxieties on him. Hand him your heavy load, let him wash your sore feet, and admit that you can't get out of eternal suffering on your own. The God who suffers alongside you can surely be trusted to bear you up! And indeed, when you humbly look to him in your suffering and rely on him, he promises to exalt you to heaven—where you'll have an eternity without suffering.

Suffering Savior, humble me and help me to trust in you for eternal life. Amen.

La Crosse, WI

Photo by: Austin Miller

GENESIS 8:22

"While the earth remains, seedtime and harvest, cold and heat, summer and winter, day and night, shall not cease."

One of the great pleasures of being outdoors is getting a clear look at God's creation. You don't have to be climbing in the Rocky Mountains, wading in the ocean, or sleeping under a million stars to be able to truly appreciate the world God made. You can be walking in a local park, hiking in a state forest, or even sitting on your front porch—every inch of God's creation is incredible! Bend down, and examine a blade of grass. Reach out, and touch the bark of a tree. Look up at the blue sky above you. Even these common features of creation tell us much about God!

These features express God's love for and providence over his creation. "He upholds the universe by the word of his power" (Hebrews 1:3). Grass provides food for some animals as well as cover and protection for others. Bark keeps a tree's water and nutrients in and animals, insects, and diseases out. Contained in the atmosphere is the oxygen necessary for all human and animal life, and the CO_2 needed for all plant life; on top of that, the atmosphere protects against the harmful radiation of the sun and helps to regulate the earth's temperature. And these are just a few of countless examples of God caring for the world he made. Isn't it incredible how God provides for his creation? Seeing this providence can remind you that God has also provided for human beings in an even more important way. God saw that, by their sinfulness, humankind brought eternal death upon themselves (Isaiah 59:2). Yet God looked down in love and provided for people a way out of death and hell, a way to eternal life in heaven! He gave his Son, who came into his own creation and subjected himself to the death that covers it (Philippians 2:8). He did this in order to defeat death; indeed, he rose again three days later! Now he offers you the greatest of his many gifts—living forever with him in paradise. You receive this gift simply through trusting that he has indeed done this for you.

Stop for a moment, look around, and appreciate how God provides for his beautiful creation—including you! As you do, be reminded and comforted that he has ultimately provided you with eternal life through his Son, Jesus!

Dear God, thank you for your provision now and eternally. Amen.

La Crosse, WI

Photo by: Austin Miller

EXODUS 3:8

"And I have come down to deliver them out of the hand of the Egyptians and to bring them up out of that land to a good and broad land, a land flowing with milk and honey, to the place of the Canaanites, the Hittites, the Amorites, the Perizzites, the Hivites, and the Jebusites."

It's hard to picture a camping trip with no campfire. In fact, my favorite thing about camping is simply sitting around a fire with friends or family, cooking dinner, making s'mores, and cracking jokes. There's just something about a fire that seems to fuel good conversation—the laughs are longer, the thoughts are deeper, and the spirits are higher. Without a doubt, many strangers have quickly become friends and many friends have turned into best friends as they've bonded around the warm, orange glow of a good campfire.

The Bible tells of another important relationship forged out of a fire: that between God and the Israelites. The setting of Exodus 3:8 is God talking to Moses out of a burning bush. Through that fire, God explained to Moses that he had seen the afflictions of the Israelites, and that he planned to deliver them from their captivity and lead them to a beautiful, abundant land, which they would possess. In that fire, God revealed to Moses the relationship he has with his people—one of care, protection, and incredible love. In that fire, Moses came to trust in God, and he became the instrument through which God brought deliverance to his people. While amazing in itself, this relationship and deliverance were also a foreshadowing of the ultimate deliverance Jesus would later bring (Hebrews 4:8). He did this by coming into the world as a descendent of those Israelites, dying on the cross to forgive sin, and rising from the dead to defeat death. By his actions, you, who were cut off from God because of your sinfulness, have been offered forgiveness and heaven! When you receive this gift through faith in what Jesus did, God says, "I will come in to him and eat with him, and he with me" (Revelation 3:20).

That's right, because of what Jesus did, you have a friendship with God! Isn't it unthinkably amazing that the God of the universe wants a friendship with you? And this is an eternal relationship! I don't know if there'll be campfires in heaven, but I do know that by believing that God has delivered you through Jesus, you'll spend eternity in the warm, glorious glow of your Heavenly Father and Friend (Revelation. 21:23).

Heavenly Friend, thank you for offering me a wonderful, eternal relationship with you. Amen.

Washington

Photo by: Austin Miller

MATTHEW 7:14

"For the gate is narrow and the way is hard that leads to life, and those who find it are few."

I've been on easy, medium, and hard hikes. Undoubtedly, my favorites are the hard ones. Long, arduous hikes present an enjoyable challenge that give a sense of accomplishment when completed. Treks away from the popular, easy trails offer an adventure that fewer have experienced. Hikes with big elevation gains lead to superb views! One of my favorite difficult, off-the-beaten-path hikes was in the White Mountains of New Hampshire. After a challenging hike up, up, up, we came to the summit and looked out over miles of tree-covered mountains—breathtaking!

What's true of hiking is also true of life: the trail to the summit is long and difficult, but it's absolutely worth it. This is what Jesus teaches in Matthew 7. Many people think that Christianity promises to fix life's problems, but actually the opposite is true—the Bible promises suffering. The world offers many shortcuts and easier paths. But they don't lead uphill to the summit; instead, they lead downward into hell. There's only one real path to the top—that trail is Jesus himself (Hebrews 10:19–20). You're called to struggle up this hard, narrow way in faith—trusting that Jesus died to become your path and that he rose from the dead to prove that he is the way. Just as he blazed the trail by his suffering, so you'll suffer up it, too. You'll struggle to evade the alluring temptations attempting to pull you off the path (2 Peter 2:1–2). You'll suffer as the devil tries to injure you and obscure your route (1 Peter 5:8). You'll labor as you carry the burdens of others (Galatians 6:2). It isn't easy. But it is entirely worth it! Paul exhorts you to "hold fast to the word of life, so that in the day of Christ [you] may be proud that [you] did not run. . .or labor in vain" (Philippians 2:16). For at the end of the hard, narrow path is eternity in an unimaginable paradise where there will be no more struggle, suffering, or toil.

The next time you take a difficult hike knowing the end will be worth it, remember the same is true of life. Jesus suffered to become for you the one way; trusting in him, you will reach the heavenly summit. By his strength, continue along this difficult path knowing that the end is absolutely worth it!

Savior, help me to struggle up the narrow, hard path to you. Amen.

Oregon Coast

Photo by: Austin Miller

PSALM 8:3-4

"When I look at your heavens, the work of your fingers, the moon and the stars, which you have set in place, what is man that you are mindful of him, and the son of man that you care for him?"

The enormity of God's creation continually astounds me. I've had the pleasure of hiking on the coasts of Maine in the east and Washington in the west. I've cliff-dived off the northern shore of Michigan's Upper Peninsula and canoed the southern tip of Florida. And I've been many places in between. The diversity of landscapes, vegetation, and wildlife is mind-boggling! And that's just one nation of the hundreds on planet earth. Widen your view even further and consider the size and scope of the cosmos; it's literally impossible to fathom! Viewed from light-years or nanometers, it's packed with design, diversity, and capacity that defy all understanding.

Considering this, David wrote in Psalm 8, "What is man that you are mindful of him?" Although there is an incomprehensible multitude of things in his creation that he could care more about, God is most mindful of human beings. Man is the pinnacle of his creation (Genesis 1:26)! That should make you feel incredibly valuable. But that's not all. When humanity fell from grace by sinning, God couldn't bear the thought of his beloved people languishing forever in hell. So, he did something truly incredible—he redeemed mankind by shedding his own blood. God gave his life so that you can have eternal life! Peter writes, "You were ransomed...with the precious blood of Christ" (1 Peter 1:18-19). Doesn't that make you feel invaluable? After all, what could be more valuable than the life of God? God's own answer is: "You!"

The next time you're enjoying God's creation, stop and look around. See every blade of grass, every rock, and every tree. Hear every scurrying squirrel, every chirping bird, and every rustling leaf. Look at every star in the night sky. Take it all in and be reminded that God loves you more than all of it. Even more, be reminded that God cherishes you above even his own life! Jesus died so that your sins would be forgiven, and he rose from the dead to give you eternal life (1 Thessalonians 4:14). Just as you can't comprehend the enormity of God's creation, neither can you fathom the extraordinary magnitude of his love for you. Know the worth he places upon you and rejoice in him!

God of love, thank you for creating and redeeming me. Help me to always find my value in you.
Amen.

Olympic Natl. Park, WA

Photo by: Rob Schrader

JOHN 4:13-14

"Jesus said to her, 'Everyone who drinks of this water will be thirsty again, but whoever drinks of the water that I will give him will never be thirsty again. The water that I will give him will become in him a spring of water welling up to eternal life.'"

Without a doubt, the most important thing to consider when beginning a long hike is how much water will be needed. Calculations are done: How many miles? How much elevation gain? How hot will it be? Will you need a water filtration or purification system? Experienced hikers consult a map when planning a multiday route—will there be adequate sources from which to replenish the water supply? Why all of this concern? Water is that important! Next to oxygen, it's a human's most fundamental need. We don't survive very long without water.

Then along comes Jesus claiming to have water that, if drunk, would satisfy thirst forever. Just think how much lighter your pack would be if only you had a drop of that water! I don't know about you, but I would pay a pretty penny to have what Jesus offers. But the "water" that Jesus refers to won't exactly keep you hydrated—rather it does something much greater. And amazingly, it doesn't cost you a dime! Jesus isn't talking about H2O; instead, he's talking about himself: he is the "spring of water welling up to eternal life." In fact, he is life itself: he created life, and he offers eternal life (John 1:4). John says, "He is the true God and eternal life" (1 John 5:20). Yet, he came down to earth in order to give up his life—he died on the cross so that you would be quenched, so you would have his life! In fact, he did it to offer eternal life to the whole world.

You see, you actually do have a need even more fundamental than oxygen or water. Because you're a sinful person, and the punishment for that sin is death and hell, your greatest need is for deliverance from this disastrous fate (Romans 5:12). And that's exactly what Jesus gives! He died to forgive your death-causing sins, and he rose from the dead to defeat death! He offers you his eternal life, and it's received simply by trusting in what he has done (Romans 4:24–25). When you trust in Jesus, you will be physically thirsty again, but your inner, spiritual thirst will be forever quenched. In Christ, you have everlasting joy, satisfaction, and love—there's nothing more wonderful than that!

Wellspring of Life, thank you for quenching my spiritual thirst. Amen.

Crater Lake Natl. Park, OR

Photo by: Austin Miller

MARK 4:39

"And he awoke and rebuked the wind and said to the sea, 'Peace! Be still!' And the wind ceased, and there was a great calm."

13

Spending time outside in God's creation is usually a pleasurable, relaxing occasion; however, anyone who has camped in a windstorm, hiked during a thunderstorm, or climbed a mountain only to get caught in a blizzard knows that's not always the case. I hope you've never experienced something even worse such as a tornado or hurricane. Even if you haven't faced these storms head-on, you still must respect their incredible power. We've all seen images of trees blown down by wind, cities flooded by tsunamis, and streets cracked by an earthquake. In these natural disasters, we're confronted with the incredible power of nature.

Mark 4 explains that the disciples found themselves in such a situation. A great storm had blown up on the Sea of Galilee, and they were sailing a boat in the middle of it. Fearing for their lives, they ran to Jesus and begged him to help. With death imminent, they feared the strength of the wind, rain, and waves around them, yet they were with someone who is even stronger. Jesus simply spoke to this raging storm—he rebuked it as a parent scolds a misbehaving child. At once, that powerful wind, those roiling waves, that deadly storm ceased—to the extent that "there was a great calm." Just as God spoke to create the world, his speech still has power over it. If you're going through a "storm" right now in life, think about how Jesus can calm raging storms and know that he can calm your life, too. He comforts by reminding you: "All authority in heaven and on earth has been given to me" (Matthew 28:18). Still, there is an enemy even stronger than storms: death. Everyone constantly lives with this most powerful of enemies ever threatening them. Is Jesus more powerful even than death? Yes! Though he allowed himself to die on the cross, "it was not possible for him to be held by it" (Acts 2:24). Just as he ended the storm, Jesus rose back to life and defeated death—that's how powerful God is! He now gives his victory over death to all who believe—that's how loving God is (John 5:21)!

As you think about and trust in Jesus's care and power, allow him to bring peace and calm to the storms of your life.

Powerful God, through life's storms, keep me in your constant, eternal protection. Amen.

Yosemite Natl. Park, CA

Photo by: Rob Schrader

PSALM 102:25-26

"Of old you laid the foundation of the earth, and the heavens are the work of your hands. They will perish, but you will remain; they will all wear out like a garment. You will change them like a robe, and they will pass away."

14

In Yosemite National Park there's a famous rock called El Capitan; when you see it, you understand why it's famous. It's huge and imposing—a strong, firm stone that rises three thousand feet straight up from the Yosemite Valley floor. Picnicking beneath it, I got the sense that El Capitan commands the valley—apparently the local Native Americans thought the same, as their word for it translates to "the chief." Through the ages, while water carved out the Yosemite Valley, El Capitan has stood solid and mighty—a seemingly eternal granite monolith watching over the valley below.

While this rock may seem eternal, however, the writer of Psalm 102 assures us that it's not. In our ever-changing world with its cycle of life and death, there are many impressive things that seem to go on forever: mountains, oceans, galaxies, and so forth. But none of these things have been around from forever and none of them will last for forever. Instead, it was God who "laid the foundation of the earth" and created the heavens. Only God has existed from forever. All these things will "wear out like a garment" and "will perish." Yet God "will remain"—he's eternal. While no person has existed from eternity like God, we will all exist for eternity. Unlike anything else in the universe, God made human beings with a personal spirit that lasts forever. Yet, because humanity broke away from God by sinning, everyone's eternal existence was doomed to be lived in hell. But that's not what God wanted; he intended for all people to spend eternity with him. So, the everlasting God died in your place. He took the punishment that you deserve for your sins so that you're forgiven! Having your sins wiped out means that if you have faith, you'll live forever with God just as he had originally planned (Hebrews 10:18-19). Jesus even assures you that he was crucified so "that whoever believes in Him may have eternal life" (John 3:14-15).

When the seemingly stout, immortal things of this universe make you feel mortal, remember that you'll actually outlive them all. You're eternal! And when you trust in Jesus' death and resurrection, then you'll be spending that eternity in paradise with him.

Eternal God, thank you for dying and rising to grant me eternal life with you. Amen.

Glacier Natl. Park, MT

Photo by: Austin Miller

amazon.com

SQfbJQ1qTY

Order of March 11, 2024

Qty. Item

1 **In God's Great Outdoors: Devotions for Hikers, Campers, and Nature Lovers**
Schrader, Rob --- Paperback
1666757721
1666757721 9781666757729

Return or replace your item
Visit Amazon.com/returns

0/QfbJQ1qTY/-1 of 1-//DWA2-CART-B/next-1dc/0/0312-22:00/0312-03:49   **SmartP**

JOHN 14:6

> "Jesus said to him, 'I am the way, and the truth, and the life. No one comes to the Father except through me.'"

Before a trip to Glacier National Park, I had meticulously planned out all our hikes using the park map. One day, two friends and I planned to hike a loop trail. Our hike was going great! Yet at one point, the trail didn't loop. We had diligently watched for our fork but hadn't seen it, yet according to the GPS we'd passed it a while ago. We decided to give up on our loop and go all the way back out the way we came in. Along the way, we passed a park ranger, and I asked about the trail. She admitted that while it was on the map, no such trail existed.

When hiking, maps are important! As we found out, if the map is wrong, you won't reach your destination. The Bible explains that it's the same with life. Most set "heaven" as their objective; however, there are many bad "maps" in existence. Many false religions claim that you can get to heaven simply by being good or by doing enough stuff. However, when you consider your sinful thoughts, words, and actions, it becomes clear that you're not good and you can never do enough (1 John 1:8). Instead, the Bible says that there's only one way to get to heaven and that's through Jesus. That's what we learn in John 14: "No one comes to the Father except through [Jesus]." Without him, you're hopelessly lost in sin, unable to walk any path but the one to hell. But Jesus came to make a way—the way. He sacrificed himself for you, taking the sins that kept you out of heaven to the cross and dying to forgive them (Galatians 1:4). That's the price that had to be paid to make the path to heaven, and that's why Jesus is the only way. You receive his eternal-life-giving forgiveness simply by trusting that Jesus has actually done this for you—that he is your one way to heaven. It's really that simple; it's really that wonderful!

Jesus gave it all so that you could have it all! If you've set heaven as your destination, make sure you consult the right "map"—read the Bible and learn for yourself about Jesus. He's the true God who loves you so much that he gave his life to become the way—your Way—to heaven!

Jesus, thank you for being my path to heaven.
Help me to walk it. Amen.

La Crosse, WI

Photo by: Austin Miller

MATTHEW 7:24

"Everyone then who hears these words of mine and does them will be like a wise man who built his house on the rock."

Anyone who has gone camping understands the importance of choosing a good place for a tent. Which place is most sheltered? Which ground is softest? Are there dangerous limbs above? A friend of mine often jokes about a campsite I unwittingly chose off the internet that happened to be one big rock. He found it difficult to pitch the tent because there was no place to drive in the stakes—which were necessary because the forecast called for wind and rain all weekend. When I arrived a few hours later, however, I was quite happy to find our tent set up on a rock; the higher ground kept us dry and stable through the next couple days of bad weather.

It's this type of setup that Jesus is talking about in the verse above. When wind, floods, and storms come, it's beneficial to have your tent or house set on a solid foundation. Of course, this is a metaphor for life—the tent or house is a person's mental and spiritual well-being, and the storms are the difficulties that people so often face in this life. If you've based your well-being on money, what happens when you're laid off? If you've based it on a spouse or family member, what happens when an accident or sickness takes them? People rely on many things in this world: fame, friends, reputation, goods, and experiences to name just a few. The Bible calls these things "idols"—when you rely on anything but God for your mental and spiritual well-being, you make that thing a "god" in place the true God (Galatians 4:8–9). Yet, God is the only part of our lives that's truly reliable; he's eternal, completely loving, and all-powerful (2 Timothy 2:13). And he's given you the one and only thing that provides for your eternal well-being: Jesus gave his own life upon the cross so that your sins are forgiven; in doing this, he opened for you the path to eternal life (2 Timothy 1:10).

Unlike the temporary idols that people so often look to for security, God promises everlasting life to all who trust in him—and this promise is rock-solid. It offers perfect mental and spiritual well-being forever! Build your house on this rock that is Jesus Christ and receive his absolute assurance of full life now and eternally.

Dear Jesus, help me to trust you only for my well-being. Amen.

Upper Peninsula of Michigan

Photo by: Austin Miller

PHILIPPIANS 2:3

"Do nothing from selfish ambition or conceit, but in humility count others more significant than yourselves."

17

I love hiking for the views, the nature, the exercise, and the challenge. But I also love hiking because of the people. I've often said that hikers are some of the nicest people you'll ever meet. Rarely have I encountered someone on the trail who isn't joyful, friendly, and willing to help. Often, others have gone out of their way to give me directions, share their water, snap a photo of my friends and me, or offer encouragement. Of course, having been shown this incredible kindness so often, I try to do the same for others.

The kindness that hikers so often show is an example of how Christians are always supposed to live. The Bible says, "Through love serve one another" (Galatians 5:13). Christians are told to sacrifice their time, gifts, and money to help those in need (1 Timothy 6:18). They're exhorted to give and expect nothing in return (Luke 6:35). They're encouraged to humbly see others as more significant than themselves (Philippians 2:3-4). Yet these moral teachings are true of most religions; they're not unique to Christianity. What is distinctive, however, is what's behind these actions. Christians act generously not to earn good karma, pleasant vibes, or some version of "heaven." Instead, they're called to serve humbly because they've already been given heaven (2 Corinthians 8:8-9)! "We love because He first loved us," John writes (1 John 4:19). How have we been served and loved? The Bible explains that even though all people are sinful and set against him, God came to earth as Jesus for one purpose: to experience the Father's wrath in place of mankind, who deserved it! Even though he lived a perfect life and was always good and kind, Jesus was accused and put to death on the cross. There he took man's sin upon himself, was forsaken by God, and died to forgive all people—including you! Now, he freely gives eternal life to everyone who believe this.

Isn't it incredible that God has served you in this way? Just as the kindness that other hikers have shown me encourages me to be kind to others, Jesus' sacrifice gives you the ability and every reason to love and serve those around you. Filled with his love and goodness toward you, show the same to others—not only on the trail, but in all parts of your life.

Jesus, help me to serve others as you serve me.
Amen.

Grand Tetons Natl. Park, WY

Photo by: Austin Miller

1 CORINTHIANS 9:25

"Every athlete exercises self-control in all things. They do it to receive a perishable wreath, but we an imperishable."

"You can make it; the view from the top is totally worth it!" I can't count how many times I've heard those words from other hikers. They're bound to be said on just about any hike with a view. Since good views generally imply elevation and elevation usually implies strenuous hiking, this makes sense. For many, those tough hikes are worth the reward at the end: a beautiful vista of God's creation. Yet that reward is short lived—eventually you must retrace your steps, head back down the mountain, and return to normal life.

But what if you could stay on top of the mountain and enjoy the great view forever? 1 Corinthians says that's possible. It talks about a reward that's "imperishable." Of course, Paul is talking about heaven! While he uses the analogy of an athletic contest, the hiking metaphor gets at the same thing: if you'll endure the difficulty of hiking a mountain to enjoy a brief reward, shouldn't you also be willing to endure difficulty in life to receive a reward that lasts forever? Admittedly, the "hike" to heaven takes a little longer. And certainly, this hike is difficult—being a Christian isn't easy (1 Corinthians 4:12–13). It's tough to give up your free time to serve others. It's hard to spend money helping your neighbor. It's challenging to keep God's commands when you're constantly tempted by a sinful world. Yet, Christians are called to work toward these things. Not to earn eternal life—your good acts can't cancel out your overwhelming debt of sin (Psalm 49:7 and Galatians 2:16)—but rather because you already have eternal life from Jesus! He died and rose to give you that gift. You're called to do good in response to the good that God has done for you (2 Corinthians 9:8). And acting like God in this way keeps you focused on him and receiving the reward he offers you.

Similar to what he expressed in 1 Corinthians 9, Paul also writes, "Let us not grow weary of doing good, for in due season we will reap, if we do not give up" (Galatians 6:9). Don't grow weary of living the life of faith. Even when the hike gets steep and tough, through the strength of the Holy Spirit keep focused on and faithful to God, for he'll grant you eternal life. And, without a doubt, the view from heaven is totally worth it!

Jesus, help me to endure in the faith unto eternal life. Amen.

Yachats, OR

Photo by: Rob Schrader

JOB 11:7, 9

"Can you find out the deep things of God? Can you find out the limit of the Almighty?...Its measure is longer than the earth and broader than the sea."

I've always been enamored with the ocean. I love to stand on the shore and ponder it. I think about how many people over the course of history have done the same. I wonder how many ships those waters have buoyed to a destination. I consider how many vessels lie beneath those waves. Perhaps most of all, I'm captivated by the sheer size of the ocean. What mysteries lie beneath its vast depths? What adventures await beyond its broad horizon? What thrills will be encountered upon its endless waves?

In the book of Job, Zophar the Naamathite basically says, "So you think the ocean is big and unfathomable? Well, God is even more!" Men can't hope to understand him; he's far too deep. Humanity can't expect to grasp him, he's literally limitless. If you're enamored with a limited ocean, how much more should you be captivated by the limitless God (Isaiah 40:28)? If you feel humbled next to the ocean, how much more humble should you feel next to the all-powerful God (Psalm 147:5)? He's so much bigger, so much better, and so much greater! Yet, if you think about it, you must admit that, in spite of this, you frequently challenge God. Actually, every time you sin, you're essentially declaring that you know better than him. Subconsciously, you're thinking, "God, I don't trust that your commands are what's best for me, so I'll do things my way." When you recall how intelligent and infinite God is, you can see that thinking this way is pretty foolish. Thankfully, God isn't only all-knowing and all-powerful, he's also all-loving and absolutely merciful (Exodus 34:6–7 and 1 John 4:8). The Bible explains that in order for you to receive his abundant forgiveness, you should be humble next to him and have faith. This involves knowing that he's holy and you're sinful, repenting for those sins, and trusting that God forgives you out of his boundless love (Mark 1:15). Jesus' death and resurrection is the proof of God's love—he's so serious about forgiveness that he backed it up with his life! In awe of this, Paul wrote: "The love of Christ...surpasses knowledge" (Ephesians 3:19).

When you're marveling at the vastness of the ocean, let it remind you that God is much vaster—be humbled. But also, be reminded that he holds even more love for you than the oceans hold water—be joyful!

Great God, humble me and help me to trust in you. Amen.

White River Marsh, WI

Photo by: Rob Schrader

PSALM 29:5

"The voice of the LORD breaks the cedars; the LORD breaks the cedars of Lebanon."

20

If you've ever taken an axe or even a chainsaw to a full-grown tree, you know they're not easily felled. It takes a great deal of power and energy to cut through one. These stout pillars of strength are not readily broken, even by the powers of nature. Most trees stand proud and tall through even the strongest winds and storms. If you're near such a tree, stop for a moment and admire its strength.

David, the writer of Psalm 29, understood that trees are stout and strong. He also knew, then, that if someone could break a tree, that person must be particularly mighty. This would especially be true if that person felled a tree simply using their voice. If you're alone in the woods or don't mind drawing attention to yourself, give it shot! Try to break a tree with your shouts. Undoubtedly, you don't have to try to know the outcome—you're not nearly so powerful! Yet David tells us that God is this strong—he's so mighty that he can break stout trees simply with his voice. Think about that for a moment—that's extraordinary! And of course, God is much more powerful even than that. In fact, that same voice spoke everything into existence: rushing rivers, mighty mountains, and towering trees (Hebrews 11:3). Your voice can't even cause a tree to flinch, much less create the universe. Be humbled. Consider how great God is, how awesome God is, and how powerful God is. Consider how small and weak you are by comparison and understand your place next to God. Shouldn't you respect him, listen to his commands, and submit to him? As the psalmist says, "Let all the inhabitants of the world stand in awe of him!" (Psalm 33:8). But also rejoice. Rejoice that such an awesome, powerful God humbled himself to serve you (Isaiah 42:1–4)! Rejoice that such a mighty God submitted himself to the tree of the cross on your behalf (Isaiah 53:5)!

Rejoice that God didn't use his might to smite you, but instead, out of love, he momentarily gave up his strength and died. Rejoice that he, once again, showed his might as he rose from that death and defeated it. Rejoice that, through faith in what Jesus has done, you get to spend eternity with the powerful, loving God!

Dear Jesus, humble me before your might and help me to trust your love. Amen.

Oregon Coast

Photo by: Austin Miller

MATTHEW 9:28-29

"When he entered the house, the blind men came to him, and Jesus said to them, 'Do you believe that I am able to do this?' They said to him, 'Yes, Lord.' Then he touched their eyes, saying, 'According to your faith be it done to you.'"

"Just trust me," I said. My fiancée stood on one rock and I on another—between us the dangerous rapids rushed. "You can do it; jump, and I'll catch you." Bravely, she made the leap and landed safely in my arms. No doubt, many who've journeyed into the outdoors have heard those words: "Just trust me." After all, it wouldn't be much of an adventure if there wasn't some obstacle to overcome. And overcoming obstacles always requires faith. Faith in yourself, faith in a friend, faith that a rock will hold, faith that a rickety bridge won't break—you get the point. At one time or another, we've all taken leaps of faith.

In Matthew 9, two blind men took a leap of faith; they came to Jesus to be healed. Essentially, Jesus asked them, "Do you trust me?" They answered in faith—they believed he could do the impossible and restore their sight. And he did! Jesus asks you this same question: "Do you trust me?" He asks because you also have an incurable ailment. You have sin—an infection that results in eternal death in hell (Psalm 143:2). You can't heal yourself. Without help, you'll succumb to that terrible fate. Jesus is the only person who could do something about it, and thankfully, he did do something about it! He died on the cross as your substitute. His life, the life of God, was worth enough to pay the price you owe for your sins. Peter explains: Jesus "suffered once for sins, the righteous for the unrighteous, that he might bring us to God" (1 Peter 3:18). And after dying, he rose from the dead to offer you eternal life (Acts 1:3)!

Jesus has done all of that, and now he says, "Do you trust me?" So, do you? Do you believe that he really forgives your sins? Do you believe that he really rose from the dead to win for you a resurrection from the dead? If so, he tells you the same thing he told the blind men: "According to your faith be it done to you." All it takes is trust; all it takes is faith—through that and that alone, you really receive the forgiveness and eternal life Jesus really did win for you!

Jesus, help me to trust in you more and more.
Amen.

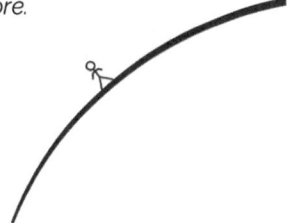

Zion Natl. Park, UT

Photo by: Rob Schrader

PSALM 19:1

"The heavens declare the glory of God, and the sky above proclaims his handiwork."

Since the beginning of time, mankind has been fascinated by the night sky. It has always evoked curiosity, study, and wonder. Sadly, with all of our light pollution and smog, we don't often get the same view of the heavens as our ancestors did. Yet, there are still remote places where you can take in the full beauty of this celestial tapestry. I experienced one such location on the shores of Lake Superior in Pictured Rocks National Lakeshore. My friends and I laid on the beach marveling at the glory of the Milky Way spread out before our eyes—it's a sight that I'll never forget!

It's this same view that inspired many ancient religions. They knew that such sublime scenery must have been created by some intelligent divinity. The Bible teaches us that, yes, these incredible starry heavens were created by the Christian God: "By the word of the Lord the heavens were made" (Psalm 33:6). This beautiful night sky is also what inspired David to pen these first words of Psalm 19. Surely, the heavens do "declare the glory of God" and "proclaim his handiwork"! The starry sky teaches man much about its creator—he's a glorious God who loves beauty, who's so powerful that he could create the universe out of nothing, and who's so intelligent that creation functions without a hitch (Isaiah 40:26). While the night sky, no doubt, shouts this message, the Bible explains so much more about this one, true God. In it, you'll find that the omniscient, omnipotent God is also your savior. The Bible explains: "God sent his only Son into the world, so that we might live through him" (1 John 4:9). That son was Jesus Christ. He offers you life through his death, by which he forgave the sins that condemn you (Colossians 2:13). And he rose from the dead to assure you that, through him, you really do have a resurrection in store (Acts 26:23)!

This is a reality more wonderful, more beautiful, and more sublime than even the clearest night sky. I encourage you to marvel at the heavens and all of God's creation. Listen as they declare to you God's glory and goodness, power and intelligence. But also let them pique your curiosity to know more about this glorious God. Turn, then, to the Bible, where God speaks to you plainly about who he is and all that he has done for you.

Glorious Creator, thank you for revealing yourself to me. Bring me to know you better. Amen.

Olympic Natl. Park, WA

Photo by: Austin Miller

MATTHEW 11:28

"Come to me, all who labor and are heavy laden, and I will give you rest."

I love to hike. But even more, I love what happens following a long day of hiking! After spending all day on the trail, it's wonderful to come back to camp, sit around a fire, cook up a big meal, and spend the evening talking with friends. Would you agree? The hike might leave you tired, sore, and worn out, but a campfire and a warm meal have a way of relaxing and reinvigorating a person. Yes, sir, after a long, hard day hiking the trail, it's wonderful to come back to camp for some rest.

Just like a return to camp, Jesus also promises you rest. Life can be like a hard day on the trail. Your journey is beautiful and often enjoyable—but you'll also face difficulty, adversity, and suffering. Ultimately, life will leave you tired, sore, worn out, and very much in need of rest. Jesus is that rest both in a temporal and an eternal sense. In the temporal, Jesus is always there with you. He's by your side as you struggle. He gives you strength to overcome every temptation, persecution, and suffering (Ephesians 3:16). But even more than that, he constantly provides you with the one thing in the world you can't find anywhere else: ultimate hope. Let me explain. Jesus endured the greatest struggle of all. He's God, yet he came to earth. Tempted and tried, he endured and lived a perfect life, not sinning even once! Though innocent in every respect, he was beaten, tortured, and despised. He was hung on a cross. He was forsaken by God his father. He took God's wrath, the punishment you deserve for your sinfulness, so that you don't have to face it. And though he died, he also rose from that death and defeated death! So, because of what he did, you have hope. He promises that if you believe in him and trust this work of his, then you'll also have a resurrection from your death to live in paradise forever.

Paul exclaims, "Since we have been justified by faith, we have peace with God through our Lord Jesus Christ" (Romans 5:1). "Peace with God"—the wonderful promise given to all who believe and enough rest to carry you through the difficult hikes of life. And when you reach the end of life's weary trail, you'll have ultimate rest: peace and life with God forever!

*Eternal Comforter, thank you for promising rest.
Help me to feel it now and always. Amen.*

Grand Tetons Natl. Park, WY

Photo by: Austin Miller

JOB 41:11

"Who has first given to me, that I should repay him? Whatever is under the whole heaven is mine."

I love being by the ocean. I love looking out over it and not being able to see land. I love how huge it is. I love how it puts me in perspective—it reminds me of how small I am. I've had a similar feeling hiking in the backcountry of Canyonlands National Park. It's a desert, a huge open expanse with nothing to block your view or fence you in: no trees or people, just rocks and dust. Like sitting next to the ocean, hiking Canyonlands is a humbling feeling—a reminder of how big the world is and how small I am.

Certainly, people like to feel big and important, but I think they also like to feel small and unimportant—that's why people like the desert, the plains, and the oceans. That's one reason the night sky has fascinated humankind for centuries. But why do people like this feeling? Perhaps because it's honest; it feels right because it is right. That's what God explains as he speaks to Job. Compared to God, you're tiny; you're hardly a speck in the vastness of the universe—a universe that belongs entirely to God! What could you ever really give to him? Nothing. All that you have and all that you are is what he has provided to you—you only exist because he made you (Psalm 139:13). Your time, your talents, your treasures, your being, even the faith and the trust you have in God—it's all a gift from God. You're unable to give him anything because everything is already his, and it's no gift to give someone what they already have. In this, you can see God's great grace toward you. Even though you're tiny and unable to benefit God in any way, you're not insignificant. In fact, you're the opposite—he says you're loved, prized, and valuable (1 Peter 1:18-19). Paul says, "You were bought with a price"—that price was the life of God's son, Jesus (1 Corinthians 6:20). Jesus came into this world, and he gave his own life so that you could have eternal life!

God died in your place to give you everything—to him, you are incredibly significant! Feel small and humble next to God but don't feel unimportant—remember you're so valuable that God gave his life for you!

Heavenly Father, thank you for valuing me so much. Amen.

Olympic Natl. Park, WA

Photo by: Rob Schrader

MATTHEW 24:13

"But the one who endures to the end will be saved."

The Bible has much to say about endurance and reward, and certainly, the hiker can relate. Many a difficult trail has been endured for the reward of a beautiful vista at the end. For example, once a friend and I were hiking the Highline Trail in Glacier National Park. Seven miles in, there's a spur trail up to a viewpoint—we decided to go for it. About a quarter of the way up, we began to doubt our decision: we hadn't realized this 0.6-mile trail gained nearly 1,000 feet in elevation. It was grueling! Through much laboring, shortness of breath, and soreness of muscles we endured. And, as we stood atop the Continental Divide looking over Grinnell Glacier and miles of mountains, lakes, and forests, we realized the reward was well worth the difficulty.

Life is a lot like that hike. Without a doubt, there's much suffering that you experience. In this passage from Matthew, Jesus is particularly talking about the suffering that Christians face. The Bible says, "Through many tribulations we must enter the kingdom of God" (Acts 14:22). The devil constantly tempts you; though it's difficult for you, God tells you to resist. The world is often set against Christians; though it's arduous for you, God instructs you to keep the faith (Luke 21:17). It's so much easier for you to make yourself "god"—to use your time and money to focus only on yourself and not on others as God instructs. All of these challenges come on top of the sickness, depression, ups and downs, and death that everyone experiences. As I'm sure you know, there's much to endure in this life! But with his words in Matthew 24, Jesus reminds you that it's worth it. He endured suffering to give you something worth enduring for. He came to earth, died on the cross, and rose again to give you hope. He did all of that to give you an eternal life free from all suffering!

If you're walking uphill in life right now—tired, sore, and out of breath—remember the hope and grace you have in Christ. Keep your eyes focused on him and his promise of eternal life. It will help you through your suffering now, and one day you'll stand at the summit of his heavenly mountain knowing that the struggles were completely worth enduring.

Savior, give me the strength to endure unto the eternal life you graciously give. Amen.

Banff Natl. Park, AB, Canada

Photo by: Austin Miller

PSALM 121:2

"My help comes from the LORD, who made heaven and earth." | **26**

Have you ever stared out into the ocean and felt small? Have you ever seen your reflection in a clear lake and thought about how intricately designed you are? Have you ever walked through a forest and considered how incredible it is that the material necessary to construct shelter literally grows from the ground? Have you ever stared over a field of wheat and been amazed that the food we need for sustenance simply sprouts from the earth? Have you ever taken a moment to stand in the pouring rain and marvel that this fundamental requirement for all life falls from the sky?

I ask you to think about these things and then to think about Psalm 121:2. Think about this whole world, this whole universe. Think about how huge and beautiful it is. Think about how intricate and well designed it is. Surely, a universe this massive took incredible power to create. Surely, a universe this beautiful and elaborate took exceeding intelligence to produce. Indeed, that is the case! Yahweh, the all-powerful and all-knowing Lord and God of the universe, created it all with his voice and still sustains it (Nehemiah 9:6). The world around you is an awesome testament to how magnificent God is! And Psalm 121 reminds you that this marvelous God is the one from whom your help comes. Isn't it comforting to know that the creator of the universe is your aid in times of trouble? What could you possibly have to really fear? What should you ever really worry about? The answer is nothing! Job says to God, "I know you can do all things" (Job 42:2). There is nothing more powerful than God. Yet he's not only mighty—he also loves you! In humility he died on a cross so that his love could be more fully known. And yet, not even death could hold our mighty God. He again demonstrated his great power by overcoming the grave and rising to life! In doing so, he defeated your most powerful enemies—death and the devil (Ephesians 1:20–21). And he did all this because he loves you! The all-powerful, all-knowing, and all-loving God is your help, your support, and your giver of eternal life when you trust in him (John 17:3).

As you consider this massive, intricate, and beautiful universe, know that its powerful creator is also your savior. Be comforted knowing that the all-powerful, all-knowing, and all-loving God has already redeemed you!

God, you are magnificent; help me to trust you always. Amen.

Glacier Natl. Park, MT

Photo by: Austin Miller

ISAIAH 11:6

"The wolf shall dwell with the lamb, and the leopard shall lie down with the young goat, and the calf and the lion and the fattened calf together; and a little child shall lead them."

Once a friend and I drove into Canada to do some wilderness camping. Naturally, we brought pepper spray in case we encountered a bear. But, apparently, it's illegal to bring pepper spray across the border; so it was confiscated. Without pepper spray for protection, we opted to skip the wilderness and went to Kakabeka Falls Provincial Park instead. Another time, some friends and I were driving into Glacier National Park. As we neared the parking lot, I had to slam on the brakes—right in front of our car a grizzly and two cubs sauntered across the road. As soon as we parked, my friend bought some bear spray at the gift shop!

Any experienced hiker or camper knows that if the right precautions aren't taken, wild animals can be dangerous—their strength and speed certainly deserve our prudent respect. That's why this passage from Isaiah is so striking. Wolves and leopards want to eat sheep and goats, not lie down with them. A parent would never allow their child around a lion—that's madness! Certainly, it is madness in this world, but Isaiah isn't talking about the here and now. He's prophesying about the new creation. Knowing that, isn't this a beautiful image? Isn't this a place you'd like to live? Isaiah describes a place of ultimate, unimaginable peace. A place where humans don't fear bears, wolves, or lions—where we don't fear each other. It's a place with no worries or stresses, no apprehensions, and no burdens (Revelation 21:4). God's new creation is going to be awesome! It's the perfect place: an unfathomable paradise where believers will spend forever with the God who is everything good (Revelation 21:3). And there's great news: you can live there! Peter says, "According to his promise we are waiting for a new heavens and a new earth in which righteousness dwells" (2 Peter 3:13). You can't personally do anything to get there, but amazingly, God graciously gives it to you because Jesus earned it for you. He died to forgive the sins that barred you from this paradise. He rose from the dead to defeat death so that all who trust in him will be resurrected to this new creation!

Because of what Jesus did, you'll no longer fear bears or lions; you'll no longer fear anything! Through faith, you have an eternity of peace.

Prince of Peace, thank you for winning for me a coming peaceful, perfect new creation. Amen.

Cape Perpetua, OR

Photo by: Rob Schrader

EPHESIANS 5:8

"For at one time you were darkness, but now you are light in the Lord. Walk as children of light." **28**

Have you ever hiked in the dark? It's something I don't do often. However, on one occasion my friends and I did too many hikes at Zion National Park during the day, and to reach our backcountry campsite, we were forced to hike at night. It was not overly enjoyable. Tired and hungry, we tripped, stumbled, and complained as we tried to follow the trail. When the light of morning dawned, however, we awoke to an amazing surprise. The night before, we had unknowingly hiked through some of the most beautiful scenery I've ever witnessed! On our hike back down, we enjoyed white, rocky domes; red, jagged cliffs; and a fabulous forest of pines.

Walking in the light made all the difference—a fact that's true of life as well. The Bible often compares not knowing God to living in darkness, and it's easy to understand why. If you don't know God, you don't know your creator or your purpose; you don't know his love, mercy, and grace. Life has no meaning as you trip, stumble, and curse your way toward a frightening death (Ecclesiastes 1:2). You live only for the temporary, fleeting pleasures of the body, which fail to fully satisfy. Contrarily, when you know Jesus, you're walking in the light. He gives your life meaning and purpose. He's the creator who wants a relationship with you. He offers you everlasting joy and hope because he blesses you with eternal life in heaven! Ephesians says that to "know the love of Christ that surpasses knowledge" is to be "filled with all the fullness of God" (Ephesians. 3:19). He's God who came down to earth and died to forgive the sins of darkness that weigh you down. He rose from the dead, defeating death and illuminating the path to heaven!

Believing this, you're made "light in the Lord," Paul says. He then tells you to "walk as children of the light." So, hike life's trail fully seeing your surroundings. Appreciate all that God does for you. Fully relish his creation and his plan of salvation. Feel peace, joy, and comfort knowing that he showers you with forgiveness, love, and mercy. Revel in the purpose and meaning with which he infuses your life—you know eternity in paradise awaits! Finally, reveal your Savior to others so they may hike in the light, too (Matthew 5:15).

Lord of Light, thank you for illuminating life's path; help me to fully appreciate it. Amen.

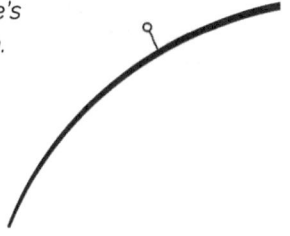

Olympic Natl. Park, WA

Photo by: Rob Schrader

ISAIAH 40:28

"Have you not known? Have you not heard? The LORD is the everlasting God, the Creator of the ends of the earth. He does not faint or grow weary; his understanding is unsearchable."

29

To touch a giant sequoia tree is to touch a piece of history. These were my thoughts as I hiked through the Tuolumne Grove in California where I was blessed to see these massive, ancient trees. Many of them are more than one thousand years old and a select few are even more than three thousand! I thought about all that they'd witnessed, all the change they'd endured, and all the challenges they'd survived. There are few living things older than these giant sequoias—they're a testament to toughness and survivability. Compared to us they seem unyielding, constant, and even eternal.

But they aren't. Winds blow them down. They perish from lack of nutrients. They burn in fires. When compared to humans they may seem eternal, but in reality, we're quite similar. Like nearly all living things, they die. I say "nearly" because there's one living being that doesn't die: God. He's existed from eternity and will exist for eternity. Giant sequoias start as a little seed, sprout, grow into a sapling, and slowly expand their height and girth over millennia until they die. But not God. He was never born, he never grew, and he'll never perish—he's the only thing that's truly constant. Moses writes, "From everlasting to everlasting you are God" (Psalm 90:2). In a way, isn't that wonderfully comforting? In a world of constant change, where disaster might strike any time, where nothing is guaranteed, where death always lurks—there is the constant, unchanging, and eternal God to cling to. And he certainly desires for us to do so. As you do, as you put your trust in the steadfast God, he gives you the certain promise of eternal life. This is an assured hope that will carry you through all the changes, disasters, and worries of life (Titus 2:11-14). Jesus won this promised hope for you in his death and resurrection by which he forgave your sins and overcame the death that kept you from him (Hebrews 6:19-20).

When you have faith in Jesus and his work for you, you can look at an ancient giant sequoia and not only know that with Christ in your heart you are stouter and stronger, but also that the tree's life is only a blink of the eye compared to what awaits you!

Steadfast God, thank you for being my certain hope in this changing world. Amen.

La Crosse, WI

Photo by: Austin Miller

PSLAM 103:11

"For as high as the heavens are above the earth, so great is his steadfast love toward those who fear him."

Without a doubt, one of the most awe-inspiring views known to mankind is that of the pure night sky. A great pleasure of camping is getting away from the lights of the city and lying out under the clear, star-filled heavens. If you've never experienced it, I highly recommend getting far away from any light pollution and going somewhere remote enough to see the Milky Way; it's breathtaking! Since the beginning of time, humans have been captivated by this view, by the heavens; their size, beauty, and brilliance have long made us feel small.

In Psalm 103, David utilizes this feeling to explain God's love to you. He uses the expanse of the heavens as a metaphor to help you understand just how huge God's love is. The farthest visible thing in the universe is more than thirteen billion lightyears away, and no doubt, the heavens expand far beyond that. That's a distance that's completely incomprehensible! Yet, it's to that, that David compares God's love. Truly, God's love is incomprehensible—it's far beyond anything you could ever hope to understand. Let me explain. God should hate you because you've turned against him. Your "iniquities have made a separation between you and God" (Isaiah 59:2). He provides for you and has given you every good thing you have, yet you reject him, blame him, deny him, spite him, and so forth. Without a doubt, God should hate you. But he doesn't. Contrarily, He loves you with a massive love! He loves you so much that he came to earth as Jesus in order to live among his creation. He loves you so much that he took all your many sins upon himself (2 Corinthians 5:21). He loves you so much that he paid the price for all that sin by dying an incredibly painful death on a cross (Romans 5:8)! He did all of this for you because he loves you so much that he wants to spend eternity with you. That is truly an enormous, inconceivable love!

When you get a chance, go somewhere dark and look up at the night sky. Think about how enormous it is and remember that God's love for you is even bigger, even more incomprehensible.

Dear Jesus, thank you for your inconceivably great love! Amen.

Wichita Mtns. Wildlife Refuge, OK

Photo by: Rob Schrader

JAMES 4:14

> "Yet you do not know what tomorrow will bring. What is your life? For you are a mist that appears for a little time and then vanishes."

One of the most unique landscapes I've ever hiked is the Wichita Mountains in Oklahoma. It's an extraordinary mixture of prairies and mountains, lakes and rivers, rapids and waterfalls. On one of my morning hikes there, a dense fog covered the terrain. The already unique surroundings took on an eeriness in the mist that made the hike exceptional. Early in the hike, I stopped often to take pictures of scenes that wouldn't last long—as the sun rose higher, the fog would surely disappear.

James explains that our lives are a lot like that fog: there for a short time, then gone. During the hike in the Wichita Mountains, the mist actually hung around quite a while. Yet other times, fog remains only a few moments and then vanishes. Either way, no mist lasts forever, and no life lasts forever. James teaches, then, that in and of themselves, human lives are ultimately short and insignificant. No matter how much money one makes, power one possesses, fame one gains, or accomplishments one achieves, everyone dies, and all that one possessed comes to nothing. Solomon writes of life: "Vanity of vanities . . . all is vanity" (Ecclesiastes 12:8). So, is your life doomed to this fleeting, trivial fate? By the grace of God, no! Though on your own you're insignificant, because of Jesus you're offered exaltation, ultimate glory, and even eternal life (John 17:3)! Jesus is God, yet he became a man, humbling himself to exalt you. He suffered the shame of torture and crucifixion to glorify you (Hebrews 12:2). He gave his life on the cross to give you eternal life! All of that gives you real significance. All of that gives your life real meaning. All of that ensures that you're no longer a vanishing mist but instead a child of God who will go on forever (John 1:12–13)! Incredibly, the Bible explains that you receive all of this simply by faith, which is trusting that God freely gives you these gifts (Romans 5:1).

Humbly consider how, on your own, your life is as fleeting as a mist. Then remember that you're not on your own—you have a relationship with Jesus, and he gives you ultimate significance and everlasting life.

Jesus, help me to find my significance in you.
Amen.

Glacier Natl. Park, MT

Photo by: Rob Schrader

GENESIS 1:31

"And God saw everything that he had made, and behold, it was very good. And there was evening and there was morning, the sixth day."

If you're outside, stop reading for a moment. Look up; look down; look all around. Take it all in and appreciate the beauty. Aren't you amazed? From the smallest blade of grass to the largest tree, from the tiniest drop of dew to the longest river—the earth is full of purpose, beauty, design, function, symmetry, and pure wonder! People stare at paintings in museums and marvel at their beauty, but nearly every painting is a rendition of something that was created by God. The natural world is far more stunning than any painting could ever hope to be. Enjoy it; love it; marvel at it!

But remember that what you're looking at is a mere shadow of the real thing. The creation you're seeing isn't God's original creation. What you currently admire has been ruined by the fall into sin, which took a mighty toll on this world. Nature is marvelous, but in its current state, it's far from the "very good" that God initially labeled it. Isaiah explains, "The earth lies defiled . . . for they have transgressed the laws" (Isaiah 24:5). So, is all hopeless? No! The Bible says that God is going to destroy this fallen, damaged world and recreate it so that it's once again "very good" (Isaiah 65:17). No more death, no more ugly decay, no more debilitating disease, no more mosquito bites! Jesus did what it took to fix this world: he died to forgive the sins that ruined it, and he rose to defeat the death that has completely overrun it. Are you excited about this new creation? I hope so, because God has promised that all who believe in him will get to live forever with him in this once-again-perfect world (Romans 8:11 and Revelation 21:3). I once told some students, "If you've seen the Grand Canyon, you've seen one of the most beautiful things on earth. But that's nothing compared to the new creation—then there'll be the Grander, no, the Grandest Canyon!"

Continue to marvel at the present natural world and appreciate how beautiful and wonderful it is. But when you do, remember that God has something even better in store for all who believe in him—look forward to that and praise God!

Heavenly Father, thank you for promising to me a new, perfect creation! Amen.

Olympic Natl. Park, WA

Photo by: Austin Miller

PSALM 112:4

"Light dawns in the darkness for the upright;
he is gracious, merciful, and righteous."

If you've ever endured a bad experience sleeping in a tent, you can certainly understand how welcoming dawn can feel. On one occasion, I was backpacking with two friends in Zion National Park. It was past dusk and reaching our destination was hopeless. Worse yet, there was no good spot to pitch a tent nearby. Eventually, we set one up right on the trail—and we quickly learned that three grown men don't fit comfortably in a two-person tent! What little sleep we got was fitful; the tent even collapsed on us twice during the night. When dawn finally broke there was certainly rejoicing! As the sun appeared on the horizon, it brought with it sufficient warmth for us to leave our sleeping bags and enough light for us to continue our hike.

The writer of this Psalm uses this welcoming feeling of dawn to illustrate the Christian life. Right now, we live in a dark world. There's sin and depravity in everyone (Psalm 14:2-3). The effects of sin are also seen everywhere: natural disasters, diseases, pain, injuries, and, worst of all, death (Genesis 3:17-19 and Romans 8:22). When you take a good look around you, you see there's a whole lot of suffering and hopelessness in this world. Maybe you've experienced some yourself. If there were no God, this life of suffering would only end in a hopeless death. But the good news is that there is a God—a loving God! While life is dark and death darker still, believers in Jesus can see light dawning on the horizon. Christians know that God loves humankind so much that he sent his only Son, Jesus Christ, to take away the dark sins of the world by dying on a cross. Jesus then rose three days later and defeated death!

Just as the dawning sun brings light to the path, warmth to the body, and the hope of a better day, the Son enlightens the path to heaven; the Son warms believers by his love and grace; and the Son gives Christians certain hope over this hopeless, dark world (1 Peter 2:9). If you're struggling right now, know that the dark night of earthly life is not forever. The light of forever in heaven is God's promise to you!

Thank you, Jesus, for giving me bright hope by your death and resurrection. Amen.

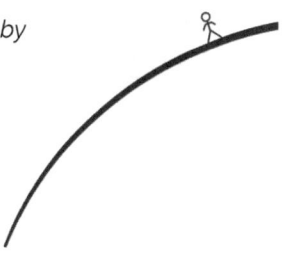

South Dakota

Photo by: Austin Miller

EPHESIANS 2:4-5

"But God, being rich in mercy, because of the great love with which he loved us, even when we were dead in our trespasses, made us alive together with Christ—by grace you have been saved."

34

I walked along the edge of White Rim Canyon deep in Canyonlands National Park hoping to find a way down. Finally, I found a route that looked dangerous, but possible, so down I went. My hike through the canyon was wonderful, but soon I had to head back to my friend and our campsite. I started climbing. Near the top, I grasped a rock and began to pull myself up, but the rock crumbled. Falling backward, I knew it was about twenty-five feet until I would hit anything. I thought, "This is it—I'm going to die."

Well, obviously I didn't. I landed on sloped gravel rather than flat rock. There was enough give in the gravel that, other than some minor injuries, I was just fine. I believe that God saved my life that day. Have you experienced anything like this: a moment you thought might just be your last? In reality, any moment could be your last. No one knows when they'll die, but it's certain that everyone will (Psalm 89:48). You might die tomorrow or in many years, but in the grand scheme of eternity, there's really no significance to the length or success of your life (Ecclesiastes 2:9–11). Even if you lived long and gained the world, it would be ultimately inconsequential—for all eventually perish, and no one can take anything along (Psalm 90:10 and Matthew 16:26). There's only one thing that gives life real, ultimate significance: faith. Faith changes everything! When I fell off the cliff that day thinking death was imminent, I wasn't afraid because I have faith. I trust that by the love and grace of God, I've been made eternally alive through the death and resurrection of Jesus. Whether I had died that day or in sixty years, it doesn't matter much because the result is the same: I'm going to heaven! Paul even exclaims that for the believer "to die is gain" (Philippians 1:21).

Jesus didn't just die and rise to save me, he did it to save you, too. Through faith, you have eternal life! You can live this life unafraid of death. You can live knowing that when you die, you'll gain. You can live with real significance because "by grace you have been saved" unto eternal life with God!

Gracious God, thank you for giving me the sure hope of eternal life through your grace. Amen.

Glacier Natl. Park, MT

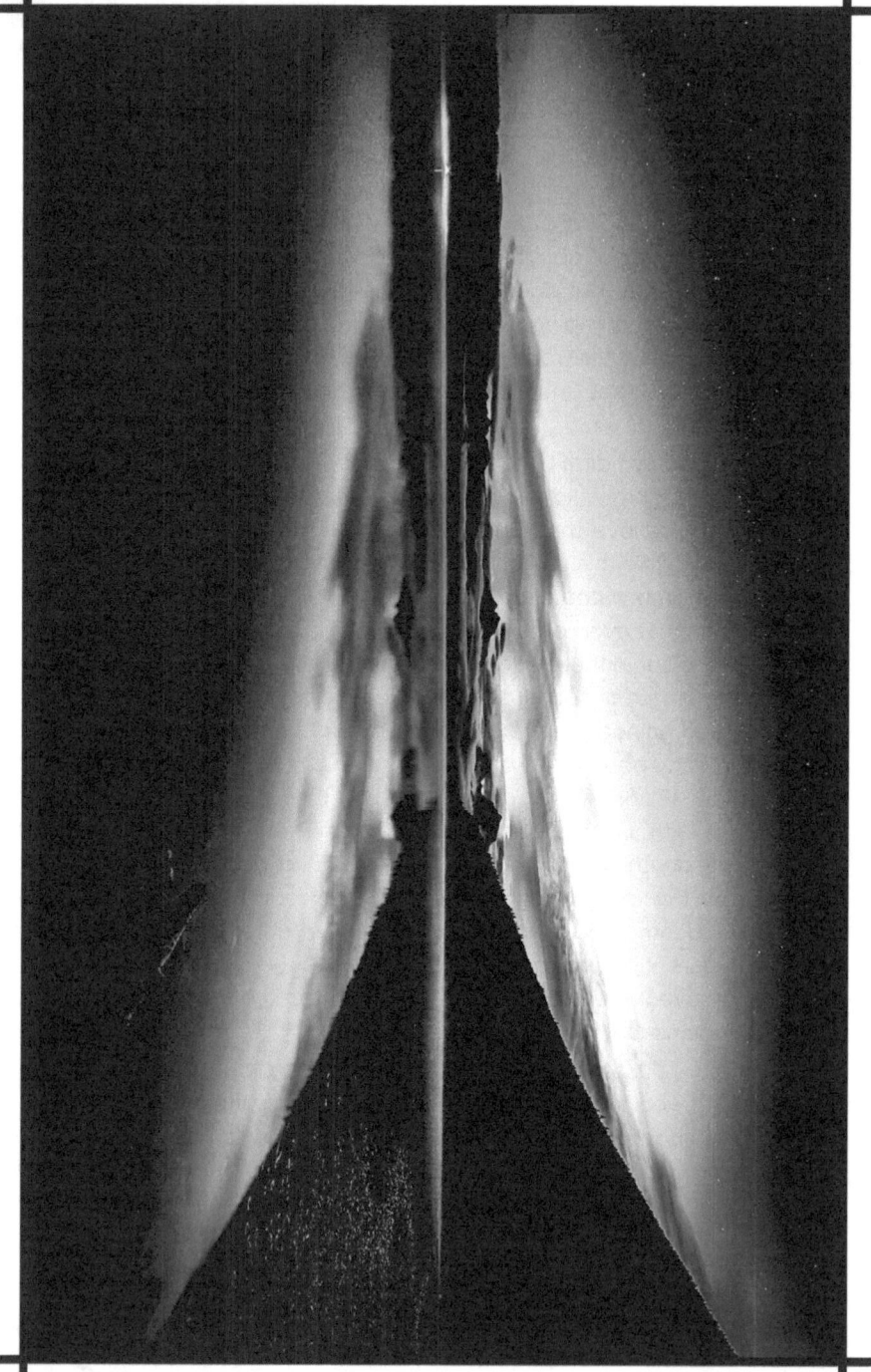

Photo by: Austin Miller

PSALM 95:4-5

> "In his hand are the depths of the earth; the heights of the mountains are his also. The sea is his, for he made it, and his hands formed the dry land."

Early one spring, I went alone to camp and hike at Copper Falls State Park in Wisconsin. I remember sitting on a hill opposite the falls, amazed by their beauty and power—God created that! I remember walking through the snowy woods feeling as if God was right there with me. I was touched by the thought that Jesus, who is God, died upon wood from a tree just like those surrounding me. I remember staring out over a horseshoe bend in the river, talking to God.

That experience at Copper Falls sticks in my mind as a particular moment when I felt very close to God. But, in fact, that's how nature often makes me feel. Considering Psalm 95, that's really no surprise. This text reminds readers that all of creation is God's. The deepest and tallest parts of the planet, the seas and all of the land, are his "for he made it." If you're outside right now, slowly turn and look. God made all that, and it's all his! Is it any wonder that people often feel close to God in nature? He personally designed and manufactured every rock and tree, lake and river, mountain and valley, and this is true of the entire universe! John writes, he "created heaven and what is in it, the earth and what is in it, and the sea and what is in it" (Revelation 10:6). Every atom in every molecule that makes up every single component in all the cosmos was engineered and created by God! This also includes you. You're "fearfully and wonderfully made" (Psalm 139:14). God shows his personal love for you by engineering and creating you. Yet, this displays only a fraction of his love—it leaves the story incomplete. His full love for you is shown most completely in the cross of Jesus. There, God sacrificed his son in order to forgive your sins and so that you could receive eternal life!

As you look at God's creation, you may feel close to him; you may even feel his love. But don't fail to look also at his cross to truly see God's surpassing love. Through it, God most clearly shouts: "I love you."

Loving Creator, thank you for loving me enough to create me and redeem me! Amen.

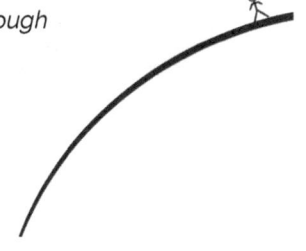

Olympic Natl. Park, WA

Photo by: Rob Schrader

JEREMIAH 17:7-8

"Blessed is the man who trusts in the LORD, whose trust is the LORD. He is like a tree planted by water, that sends out its roots by the stream, and does not fear when heat comes, for its leaves remain green, and is not anxious in the year of drought, for it does not cease to bear fruit."

Have you ever seen a tree like the one mentioned in Jeremiah 17? It's a beautiful sight to behold. Once, I was hiking in the desert of Canyonlands National Park in Utah; in one particular section, there were no trees. I don't mean there were few trees, I mean there were absolutely no trees for miles in any direction. Yet deep down in a little traveled canyon, I saw it—a lush green tree. Incredible! Why there? Well, when the rare rain falls, all of the water flows to that lowest point, and enough moisture gathers there for that tree to flourish.

When a tree's roots are connected to life-giving water, it thrives; when they're not, it dies. Jeremiah explains that it's the same for people. If your purpose, hope, and fulfillment are rooted in the temporal things of this world, they wither when those worldly things go away. Life becomes a meaningless struggle for satisfaction lived under the impending threat of death. But Jeremiah explains that if you're rooted in the life-source of Jesus, this is not so. Like that tree in the desert, you can flourish! You'll have purpose as you live for the God who lived and died for you. You'll have hope as you trust in God to give you eternal life and to bring you freedom from the worry that's so prevalent in this transitory world. You'll have fulfillment as you're filled with the absolute promise of eternal life in heaven! "The fear of the Lord leads to life, and whoever has it rests satisfied" (Proverbs 19:23). This satisfied rest comes entirely from the cross of Jesus Christ. It's there that your sins were paid for by the precious blood of God incarnate. It's there that the great exchange took place—Jesus took your sins and gave you his righteousness (Hebrews 9:14)! When you believe this, you're made holy through faith and will enter eternal life in heaven (Romans 3:30).

Just as seeds not planted by water soon die, all people who have not put their faith in Jesus will perish. Rather, be rooted in Christ and you'll be rooted in eternal life itself—an abundant stream that never runs dry and fulfills forever! Then and only then, you'll flourish.

Eternal-life-giver, thank you for being my stream of eternally satisfying water. Amen.

Olympic Natl. Park, WA

Photo by: Austin Miller

PSALM 29:4

"The voice of the LORD is powerful; the voice of the LORD is full of majesty."

37

While I enjoy going hiking and camping with friends, sometimes I also enjoy doing those activities alone. Have you ever walked by yourself down a trail and started talking to God? When I'm alone with him in his creation, I naturally find myself doing just that. I feel close to God, connected to God, and almost like he's right there with me. And of course he is—he's always with his Christians. Still, there's something about being in nature that makes it feel as if he's even closer.

Perhaps that's because, as Psalm 29 explains, in a way, God talks through his creation. The rest of this psalm relates God's voice to nature: it breaks the cedars, it shakes the wilderness, and it even makes the deer give birth. Psalm 29 explains that God works power and majesty through his voice—power and majesty evidenced by his creation. It's by his voice that God brought the universe into being. God said, "Let the earth sprout vegetation"—every blade of grass, every wildflower, and every tree around you is a result of God's voice (Genesis 1:11). "Let the earth bring forth living creatures"—every insect, every chirping bird, and every animal you come across is there because of God's powerful voice (Genesis 1:20-24). "Let the dry land appear"—that's right, even the rocks, dust, and dirt under your feet come from God's voice (Genesis 1:9). The same is true for everything you see, smell, touch, hear, and taste. The same is true for you, too—you exist because of God's voice (Genesis 1:26)! Certainly, to be in God's creation is to hear the echo of his voice.

Listen to that echo. As you experience his creation, let it remind you of his might, providence, sovereignty, care, beauty, and wisdom. Remember also that God's voice is heard most directly in the words of the Bible. In it, you'll hear him say the same things that he says through his creation and so much more! Things like, "God shows his love for us in that while we were still sinners, Christ died for us" (Romans 5:8). Indeed, you'll hear him say again and again that he loves you so much that he sent his son to give you salvation!

Almighty Father, thank you for speaking to me.
Help me to listen to your voice. Amen.

Cape Flattery, WA

Photo by: Austin Miller

1 PETER 1:6-7

"In this you rejoice, though now for a little while, if necessary, you have been grieved by various trials, so that the tested genuineness of your faith—more precious than gold that perishes though it is tested by fire—may be found to result in praise and glory and honor at the revelation of Jesus Christ."

It's no accident that some of my best friends are those with whom I've repeatedly gone camping and hiking. Strong relationships are built when striving and surviving together through the challenges, dangers, and inconveniences of the outdoors. It's with these friends I've struggled and been lost, tired, wet, and cold. It's these friends I've relied on. It's by these friends I've been encouraged. It's with these friends that I look back and laugh at those trying times. It's these friends who I know will be my friends for the rest of my life.

Peter talks about a relationship like this in 1 Peter 1. Your faith, and likewise your relationship with God, is strengthened through suffering. In fact, Peter is so serious about the benefits of suffering that he tells you to rejoice in it! When you have to rely on your hiking mate to get you through, your trust in and your relationship with that person is strengthened. Likewise, when you struggle here on earth and rely on God to get you through, your trust in and relationship with him is strengthened. When you face obstacles that you can't overcome alone, God gives you strength. When you despair, God gives you hope. When you're weighed down, God bears your burden (Psalm 68:19). But how can you be certain that God is always there to help? Well, it's because he also went through suffering and struggle. God knows what it's like to face obstacles—he faced the cross. God knows what despair looks like—he faced the cross. God knows what it's like to be weighed down—he bore the sins of mankind on the cross (1 Peter 2:24). There he suffered. There he died. There he gave it all so that your suffering-causing sins are forgiven, so you can be reunited with God, and so you can have an eternity free from suffering.

When you suffer, look to the suffering God for help. When you do, your relationship with and faith in him will be strengthened (Psalm 119:67). That's why Peter tells you to rejoice in suffering. Suffering strengthens faith, and faith receives eternal life with the God who relieves all suffering and gives you everything good!

Heavenly Friend, help me to trust in you for deliverance from my earthly struggles. Amen.

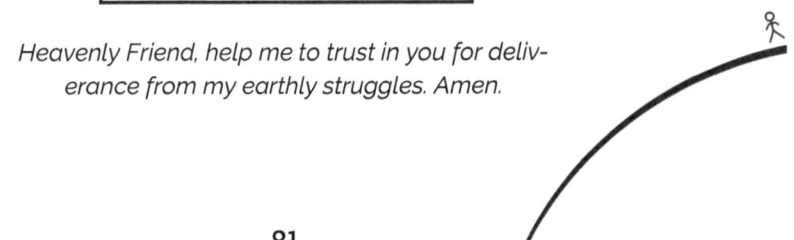

Grand Tetons Natl. Park, WY

Photo by: Austin Miller

ROMANS 1:16

"For I am not ashamed of the gospel, for it is the power of God for salvation to everyone who believes, to the Jew first and also to the Greek."

When I visit my parents after a hiking trip, my dad will often sarcastically ask, "Was that the best hike you've ever been on?" Over the years, I've told him that I've been on so many "best hikes ever" that he thinks I overstate my experience. To be fair, he's right! But that's natural—when I return from a wonderful trip, having enjoyed a piece of God's beautiful world, I'm excited and can't wait to tell people about it. So, every time I'll gather my family, show them the pictures, and tell them stories of the best trip ever.

Everyone gets excited to share good news like this. In Romans 1, Paul talks about this very thing—though his news is better than any report of a hiking trip. Paul was excited to share with people the good news about Jesus. He traveled thousands of miles, was beaten, thrown in prison, and eventually killed because he just couldn't stop telling people about Christ. Paul did this because he knew that the Gospel, which means "good news," was "salvation to everyone who believes." And he knew that to believe and thus be saved, people first had to hear the good news, so he dedicated his life to telling it (Romans 10:14). This good news about Jesus is that he is truly God, yet out of love he humbled himself to become a man (John 1:14). Out of great mercy, he endured torture, shame, death on a cross, and separation from God his father. Then, by his great power, he overcame death and rose three days later (Ephesians 1:19-20)! Because Jesus was raised, Paul explains, God "raised us up with him and seated us with him in the heavenly places" (Ephesians 2:6-7). This incredible gift of spending eternity in heaven with God is freely given to all who believe in Jesus—now that's good news! In fact, it's the best news—no other message promises nearly as much!

If you're anything like me, it's natural for you to share good news from your life but often hard to share the best news of the Gospel. Yet, filled by Christ's grace, learn from Paul. Just as you're not ashamed of your hiking, don't be ashamed of Jesus and his good news. Share this message of salvation with those around you so that they may hear, believe, and be saved also!

Jesus, help me to share your good news. Amen.

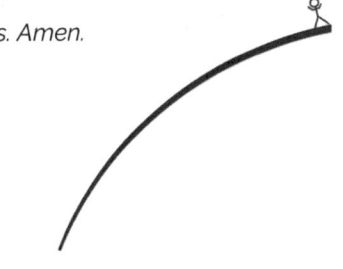

Glacier Natl. Park, MT

Photo by: Rob Schrader

JUDGES 5:5

"The mountains quaked before the LORD, even Sinai before the LORD, the God of Israel."

A few years ago, my friends and I took a road trip out to Utah to do some hiking. We drove all night through the plains of Nebraska and eastern Colorado, and I'll never forget the sight we witnessed as the sun began to rise—the incredible Rocky Mountains! Past Denver, we parked the car at a pull-off, got out, and stared at the vista of snowcapped peaks that lay before our eyes. The majesty, the enormity, and the beauty of those mountains is burned into my brain! Since then, I've been able to visit, hike, and drive through mountains several more times, but my reaction remains the same. There are few things on this earth more impressive, more beautiful, and more awe-inspiring than mountains.

Yet, Judges 5 tells us one thing that is certainly greater, grander, and far more marvelous than even mighty mountains—God. He is so much bigger and better that even the mountains quake before him. Think about that—an entire mountain range quaking simply because God is present. I have a hard time imagining it, much less fathoming the sheer awesomeness of God. Even more incredible is the fact that this God, the one who makes the mountains quake, loves you (John 3:16)! It makes sense that the God of the universe would be mighty and grand, but for that all-powerful God to also love you—well, that's something truly unbelievable. And yet, it's true. And he proved it. He loves you so much that he wants to spend eternity with you, but he couldn't because while he is perfect, pure, and holy, you're sinful, impure, and unholy (1 Corinthians 6:9-10). Still, God's love is so strong that he paid the ultimate price to earn for you eternity with him in heaven. He died on the cross; he gave his life for yours. Now, "the blood of Jesus. . . cleanses us from all sin"—in other words, you've been made pure and holy (1 John 1:7)! Three days after his crucifixion, Jesus also rose from the dead in order to give all believers a bodily resurrection unto eternal life (Romans 8:11).

Next time you see a mountain, remember that God is so great that his mere presence would make it quake—respect God's awesome power! Also remember that even though he's so mighty, he set his might aside to give his life for you. The mountain-quaking God cares for you that much!

Glorious God, thank you for being both powerful and loving enough to save me. Amen.

PSALM 148

¹ Praise the Lord!
    Praise the Lord from the heavens;
    praise him in the heights!
² Praise him, all his angels;
    praise him, all his hosts!

³ Praise him, sun and moon,
    praise him, all you shining stars!
⁴ Praise him, you highest heavens,
    and you waters above the heavens!

⁵ Let them praise the name of the Lord!
    For he commanded and they were created.
⁶ And he established them forever and ever;
    he gave a decree, and it shall not pass away.

⁷ Praise the Lord from the earth,
    you great sea creatures and all deeps,
⁸ fire and hail, snow and mist,
    stormy wind fulfilling his word!

⁹ Mountains and all hills,
    fruit trees and all cedars!
¹⁰ Beasts and all livestock,
    creeping things and flying birds!

¹¹ Kings of the earth and all peoples,
    princes and all rulers of the earth!
¹² Young men and maidens together,
    old men and children!

¹³ Let them praise the name of the Lord,
    for his name alone is exalted;
    his majesty is above earth and heaven.
¹⁴ He has raised up a horn for his people,
    praise for all his saints,
    for the people of Israel who are near to him.
    Praise the Lord!

PRAYER

Loving Creator,

When I look at your great outdoors and all that you have made, I am reminded of your power, wisdom, goodness, and love. I thank you for the beauty all around me and within me that you have created and that you have entrusted to me and my fellow man. I thank you for giving me my senses to experience these gifts. I thank you for continuing to provide for me and all that you have established.

While your creation is very beautiful and marvelous, I also see the imperfections that exist because of mankind's sin. I'm reminded of my own grievous wrongs against you, and I repent—I am humbled and sorry for my many sins. Still, the immense beauty that remains reminds me also of your goodness, renewal, and promises. Indeed, you sent your son to Earth to die for my transgressions, and he has arisen so that I too will rise when you return to recreate this world in perfect splendor! For those gifts I am most grateful! Thank you for your incredible sacrifice. Let it bring me joy, hope, peace, and love.

Lord, I pray that you continue to bless your creation. I ask that you help me to be a good steward of your world and the personal gifts that you have given to me. Finally, I pray that you would bless my time in your great outdoors today and keep me safe as I experience and enjoy your wonderful gifts!

Amen.

HAPPY TRAILS!

Made in United States
Troutdale, OR
03/11/2024